Book One

The Breath of God in Us
By
Anthony Walker

———————————

Book 1: The Breath of God In Us
Book 2: The Trinity OF God In Man
Anthony Walker

Published By Parables
January, 2020

All Rights Reserved. No part of this book may be reproduced or utilized in any form or by any means, electronic or mechanical, including photocopying, recording, or by any information storage and retrieval system, without permission in writing from the author.

    ISBN 978-1-951497-24-8
    Printed in the United States of America

Readers should be aware that Internet Web sites offered as citations and/or sources for further information may have been changed or disappeared between the time this was written and the time it is read.

Book One

The Breath of God in Us

By

Anthony Walker

PUBLISHED by PARABLES
Earthly Stories with a Heavenly Meaning

In the beginning was the Word,
and the Word was with God
and the Word was God
and the Word was manifested through the manifestation of the Word of God.

That manifests itself into that of the form of man.
That man May witness the word of God in the form of man as he walked along man.
This is why the Lord order the steps of each individual, according to the purpose that he have for that individual that is called into Christ;
When he said, let he that has eyes See, and let understanding have understand , and let hearing, hear; Hearing comes by faith, and faith comes by hearing the word of God, Who is the author and finisher of every man's faith. THE understanding of faith on Earth is Faith In Heaven that has to be constantly reminded of by the relationship with The Trinity of God in Us.
But the presence of God is the ever reminder of the practice of our faith, and gathering our faith when we are in Heavenly places, that is faith.
I love the way the Lord moved in my life for the enemy came at me one way and Scatter seven different ways;
Different ways the enemy scatter,
If we endure in the word of God to the end.
You have heard it said that you take a mold hill and make it into a mountain,while those beside you looking at a mountain the size of a molehill;
Because they cannot see it as far as you, or you may not be able to see as close as them.
The higher we go in the word of God, the Futher we see in the word of God;
So are you always conscious ?
Remindering of Him by Every Breath that comes out your nostrils ?

I could think about him for Everytime A breath come out my nostrils;

I think about him who delivered me by the showing of His hand,

Too many times, Til I am very aware of him.

I was in the shower tonight and the Lord just showed me a wonderful work. What the devil tend for evil, God showed me the good that he would manifest out of it,

And we can gain wisdom from carnal minded people, Who claim to be spiritual ;

For Jesus said ,

Everyone who says, Lord Lord, is not of me;

For everyone was not called unto me; Believing in that, that is spiritual, but don't know he that is spiritual, and that is Christ Himself.

Though it was He (the most high Jehovah) that brought us unto Him,

The blood to cleanse us, Is to purge us, to cover us, to overcome those things that come against us;

The body of Christ that abide in me and I in He,

For faith is the creative voice of God that established substance of the evidence of the things that are not seen by the carnal mind,

But seen to be spiritual, This Is to be faithful;

Greater Faith is the revelation of the manifestation of the word of God, that brings the seeing,

For you to elevate and go up into Jerusalem.

That is The heavenly dwelling place of God.

For it is the Holy Ghost that keep us in ever reminder that we are the inheritance of the power in the authority given to us unto Christ.

As the inheritance that I can keep his word as the Man and Woman of God,

That I see and so shall you be the man of God that we shall know.

Because he gave me five stones and I got unto the truth finds you out, when you commit to your walk Faithfully in the like minded in Christ.

Now you will do that, that you're faithfully in,

Because if you are changed by Him then you will be changed in Him, and you will honor your word as the Man or Woman of God,

That no-fault be found in you.

I asked the Lord;

What is it to be meek and humble?

The Prophet asked the Lord,

And the Lord said to my Lord as the Holy Spirit is speaking back unto Christ who gives it unto the Father,

That brings it back to Christ that gives it unto his servant that abides in Christ,

And what was commanded in heaven was manifested on Earth;

What's invisible was made visible to build a church and start a Ministry just like that;

Because I leaned not onto my own understanding,

But He that surpasses all understanding and bring us into that understanding; And then you get the order of the word of God.

To ask for those things by Christ and in Christ as he asked before the father Whom he is Christ,

That we abide in Christ, And I In he and he In me , For we become one in Christ walkin And and talkin for me before the Father who is also in Christ.

For this is the Father of Christ,

For We Abide in Christ for He is the only Begotten Son Of The Most High God;

For we are the Children Of The Son Of God.

For he is my friend , my confidence in myself and I'm in Christ. So the father gives also to the Son.

For (I AM) The Son Of Christ;

The only begotten son of the Father of the nation of Judith.

Those are the ones that was given to Judah by Israel That is his Name,

That govern his people by his name and he is Israel in heaven, and the Son sits on the throne of Judah.

The Children of Christ whom is Israel. we say that we judge the religions because we have not the spiritual Faith to Faith, understanding the understanding by God,

in that one and only true God that governs his many nations in the name of Jesus;

For when did God himself start covering his people that belongs to him on Earth as those that has been given to Christ on Earth?

That the children of Christ also mingle with the sons of God;

For when I bring these two Nations together,

That is the sons of God and the children of Christ, that was given by his father who is the God of Abraham, Isaac and Jacob;

Those children belongs to the most high God and his name is Israel.

So he called his Son's Israel and those that was given to Christ are named Judah. He has been given to by the father who covers his children of Christ. the sons of Christ that came into the church, that's the indwelling of Christ. understanding the Lord sends the prophet unto his church to another Prophet who's the pastor of a church, not by my word, not by his word,

But by God word who also confirm in confirmation His own word;

And that is the revelation of his word that you would see His Word if you hear his word.

For Christ Jesus said, My sheep know voice, So we Hear his word, familiar with his word.

What is His word?

His word is Parable for that is the speech of Christ, to see that this invisible be made visible.

Be not conformed to the things of this world,

Not only seeing the physical aspect of that is in the imagination of how that all came to be that .

But we see the spiritual of that's created in the spiritual, manifestsing itself in time, that we can see the physical aspect of that that's invisible made visible in heaven as it is on Earth;

Let there be light and behold you see that that was said by the words of God, in the name of Jesus,

For the voice of God is the voice of Christ.

The force of Christ who tells it into the Holy Ghost whom speaks into that substance of the things hoped for,

The evidence of the things that are unseen (The creative voice of God); Made visible that you may receive that that is invisible made visible, and that is Faith.

According to the measurement of your faith is the measurement of that that you receive.

For you cannot have lack of faith and ask for this unless God who gives the increase.

Even Greater Grace to those that is in His Mist and he would bless them with the measurements of faith that it took to receive by faith.

Only two mites that the lady put-in by faith and receive a greater reward than those who had much more.

NOT IN VAIN God moves by purpose, EVERYTHING that is created will not be wasted,

But there is a purpose, a time, And a season for everything,

To the purpose of people, places, things, situations,and/ or circumstances;

For God is not the author of confusion, confusion comes when we try to interpret the mind of God with the carnal and worldly knowledge of our carnal mind that bring in confusion. That he would make your crooked places straight out of the confusion that you even YOU get the wisdom out of the confusion that was lost among those that was in confusion.

Understanding when the Lord has told you many times to stop stop stop stop stop,

Behold A prophet comes before you, Seeing the witness,

He said let it be two witnesses in the name of Jesus listen to this, let there be two witnesses but I'm just preaching in the word.

About continuation of sin that they just talked that in Sunday School ROM. 7:14-25

when we keep going to the same Sins that Afflicts our soul when the Flesh gets weak;

And the prophet of the Lord says be real. Be real ,

So I confess my sins to him.

There's nothing you can bring to me, (NO GUILT) ROMANS 8:1

Because you are holy and you will know this is the prophet of the Lord but yet you hide your hand from God

who sent you the prophet of the Lord.

I asked the Lord what is it to be MEEK and HUMBLE?

And this is the understanding that was given into (ME)

TO BE QUICK TO HEAR AND SLOW TO SPEAK WHEN:

Humiliation opens her mouth towards you.

to be humble as a dove and wise as that serpent ,

who brings forth to humiliate,

you judge you ,

backbite towards,

you to speak ill about you and all these things that come against your temple. Because of my namesake, Because I am in you and you are in me and if they have said few things unto me,

they will also say them unto you,

for me and my father is one as I am with with you..

Humble and Meek not in time of Peace. when the opposing element of (IT) comes about. Then you will see the enemy.

The Rhema word is Revelations :

Rarely I ever get to catch this one on record,

This is a revelation from God that is given to those that holds that gift in 5th fold of the 5 fold levels of The Gift of Christ.

For all gifts that is given From God; According to the measurement of that fold, all the gifts that's given unto the five-fold Ministry and this gift is attained in the fifth fold of the ministry; And that is the apocalyptic word of God. This gift allows those that attained it by the exercising of the Holy Ghost who we received from the Lord,

To pour into us this power of the ANOINTING.

For my cup runneth over,

For your cup begins to run over when God is speaking to your spirit,

And the Lord allows us,(that). As we maintain our present physical aspect according to Time,

And the Lord give you, me and us different Revelations of these different things that attain to our personal walk in our personal life;

Even shaping and molding the understanding of our relationship being more aware in our personal life.

Even shaping and molding the understanding of our relationship being more aware of when the things of the spirit attack you through the carnal mind of The Flesh .

Not to entertain that flesh, But the

Spirit that is entertaining that flesh and you begin to react to everything different.

Because We're staying spiritual minded and we ask the Lord how do I open Ones eyes?

For an example here's a little short situation that when two people look at the same thing their outcome is how they look at it and what perspective they see it in at what rim are you discern again.

My Friend always tells me, Baby you just don't see what I see,

And it all came to pass as what she said will come to pass.

But said that I could not see it.

But to show her that I saw what she saw and reacted to my own eyesight with what you have seen and I have seen through you I also can see it so my approaches according to the will of God, not the will of man.

Because it's not the reaction you had expected according to your understanding of the sight that you have;

You can only understand the things that you see, But if I see also what you see, and see futher,

Then the Lord moves me to move accordingly according to his understanding

Not the understanding that was given to you for that end comes increase to what you had already said,

that you may ALSO see;

This is what I try to teach you.

That Even in our relationship we War not with flesh and blood, But also spirits and principalities.

If the spirits are joined together do spiritual warfare stop?

No and I know the Lord knows that we will consult him In all things,

But yet I am still flesh trying not to deal with my feelings in my emotions according in the will of God.

But allow God to control my physical emotions, That is to have joy on the inside At all times.

CHAPTER 2

(Identifying by Revelation)

(Identifying by Revelationevelation)
How can we cast something out if we don't know what we're casting out? For Jesus said who are you ?what are your name ?

And they even had to give him the truth and (legion) said there is more than one, There is a lot of us;

just to let you know that's how many it is now;

This is who we are:

And he's one that speak IT'S name out by the commandments of Jesus Christ, had to be cast out by name and identified by the physical characteristic of the spirit that operates within.

So how can you fight something you can't see? How can you name that that you have never seen? The name puts the identification of the image of that name addiction, fornication, or Manga spirit, and deceiving Spirit, Pride.

These are spirits, these are demons by name and it is integrated in your everyday life.

And it becomes carnal and not spiritual so you say this demons name all the time, and don't realize that is actually a demon.

But according to your understanding as a person who misuse, drugs, alcohol that has addiction even your afflictions you know of yourself.

This is the Revelation that I received from God to be given unto the other churches, (THE BODY OF CHRIST)

That will receive the word of God.

(Ezekiel 2nd chapter)

Thorns and thistles that he say he would send me a to such a rebellious Nation for even I have rebelled since this day have we not to sin is to rebel against God? such a rebellious Nation he sends it to his prophet even among scorpions those who try to kill the Anointing in the church these things that I speak on other things that I am actually walking through dealing with home church and my own personal life only see the things that I say the things that I see, As I walk that I speak of this day.

How can I identify the things that I am speaking this day?

That these things that I speak of this day all the things that I am involved with up to this day. My personal life to stand in the insurance of the word of God and have more than confidence but more than Faith but to be one with he who creates all faith that is the body of Jesus Christ walking after the spirit and not after the flesh but in the likeness of man but he came in the likeness of man the like me in a man is the physical aspect of that man which is called the best so that carries the temple the temple is the Heart of God that holds the body of Jesus Christ.

That is to walk in the mind of Christ
for you do as YOU see HIM do.
I see my father as you see me,
I will be one with him as you are one with me.

CHRIST spoke that in existence of the spirit of man that they can actually become one with Christ, and walk as Christ.

For you would do even greater things than these for those who can walk in Christ,

Allowing the Holy Ghost in Christ to have total control over the Temple so as the word of God is being spoken,

who was Invisible that is being spoken made visible for the physical aspect of creation on top of creation this is when the word of God moved through someone's life.

All the things that we speak on,
that I am currently in my own personal life In Jehovah,

For my cup runs over, so the Lord uses me for these things.

(How do we fight the things that we cannot see?)
How do we fight the things that we cannot see.
He will not let be ignorant,

For he seen you in the midst of confusion,
For what I have seen you also will receive Clarity that there would be no conflict nor confusion that will remain in our most.
(God is not the author of confusion but the devil is.)
God is not the author of confusion but the devil is.
But only pure Clarity of the word of God given unto thee. So I take the True way, I take the Water of Life as the woman at the well took the water of life and I go and I feed my people this Water of Life that's been given to me by Christ, But this is not a physical thing,
This is a spiritual thing, For all things were created in the spirit by him and for him.
Father this is what I want so I requested that HE create this thing in heaven and because this is how he wanted, so I walk his walk, that's the Walk of Christ. Ordered and ordained created by the Father;
Everything that happened was going to happen and was already predestined, because that was what Jesus chose to happen.
Not what man decided to do, even the lashes in the whips in the humilation. But God.
(If it be that will remove this cup not my will but thy will)
This is what Jesus said:
That's what He wanted and God created it and put it on Earth for man to see it as it is in heaven.
As it is on Earth for Jesus was crucified twice in the flesh and in the spirit that is the Revelation from God. These things that are spoken, These things that are seen.
Are we going to the church and testify by witness to the things that we have seen and heard ?
Whether it was in The Flesh or in the spirit ?
Caught up in glory and receiving much knowledge and revelation and we passed these letters out into the church for yes we too are afflicted asPeter ,John, Me, You, and,Paul is afflicted as Jesus promised that those that are chosen will be afflicted.

In our chains and in our woes and all our own battles with our flesh,
But to yield to do the word of God;
I learned to take pleasure in these infirmity, In this time when I go into the spirit weather it is in the body, I know not,
Or in the spirit I know not,
But one thing I know God Knows It's.
And weather in the spirit or in the flesh I know not, God knows .
I am caught up into paradise and I heard unspeakable things that was not even llawful for a man nor myself by his mouth nor my own according to the fleshly understanding To speak the word of God by the Flesh.
So it's given to a Elect few that's why only certain churches received the letters that Paul wrote as he received these things from divine revelation and knowledge.

CHAPTER 3

(We found pleasure).

In Our shackles and chains we found pleasure,
going into the Heavenly places and seeing the Walk of Life as it will be walked in heaven this is what the Lord show Paul And all who walks the continuation of this perfect work until Christ returns.

That the word is true, that He will deliver us even, me from my afflictions of The flesh.

To be caught up in glory in the spirit, to be with him in joy and out of the afflictions of the body, which is the despair.

To be absent from the body is to be present with God, and the word show to be true.

And We found pleasure for the body will surely die and not enter Heaven.

But I tell you what I seen:

My crown and We even I seen his crown,

I went and spoke unto Holiness, And The WORD spoke this letter:

FOR what HE bare-witness of and HE saw.

for I will be there with you in the spirit why my body is in these chains I will see you in the spirit and commune with you in the spirit, even Christ coming with us in the spirit, For did not he see the brother under the Fig Tree?

And what he was doing whilr his body was communing with his disciples?

His spirit testify to a truth that;

That one bare-witness to be true what was impossible to attain by regular Man;

This Revelation is to be ministered and Revealed, that you'll be able to see the spiritual aspect and know how to communicate with the Holy Ghost. Because you become one with the body of Christ and allow Christ to have control over your body as you yield your members over to him so I take pleasure in my infirmities that is the word.

CHAPTER 4

WHEN SATAN APPROACHES

And the Lord brought me to the wise of the devil in the understanding of when Satan approaches in the form of a light to try to persuade those that abide in the light that they're not of the light no other in the light in the Holy Spirit then quick as you in the light to bring you to the understanding in the power and authority of that is the light that is Christ that abide by the light and draws us into his marvelous like that we may not be persuaded by the devil.

And the Holy Ghost who is paraclete defends us as the children of Christ as A mighty fortress of God.

Tearing down the strongholds of the manipulation in the illuminated delusional character of Satan that we may not be snatched out of his hands for Christ lost none not one Except for he who was the son of the prediction who is the son of Satan called Judas the devil.

For our Lord and Savior Christ Jesus said that he would not leave us ignorant by the holy ghost are we brought into Divine understanding.

By the spiritual side of Christ who sees what is done by the Father who art in heaven.

When the Lord brought me to know the understanding between the deeds of the flesh and the deeds of the spirit,

I came to understand what is a physical offense to be offended by the flesh and to be offended by the spirit who comes to a offend the holy ghost that abides in, The spiritual sight of a spiritual attack that come by way of a physical distraction we see as the sin nature of the flesh.

CHAPTER 5

THE WALK.

In A Spiritual walk, one must have spiritual sight;
when you open up the scriptures that give you instructions on how to talk to the father through Christ If any man lacks wisdom let him ask fowho give in abundance and unbraided. so I asked God for that wisdom that he gives in the in abundance and unbraided.

But by Spiritual wisdom would I ask God for us so I asked the Lord;

To teach me to pray for that I know not what I ought to pray for;

And the Lord gives me then the Holy Ghost who tells me what needs to be said in that very hour, and I pray to God to ask him what I need to pray for that was given to me by the Holy Ghost. Because I asked and when you going through the scriptures, as the Lord leads you.

You are able to walk with Christ for his walk was not just physical walk, but everything that was done with Christ ,in heaven as it is on Earth; was invisible made visible for that is good. What is visible shall fade away and behold all things are invisible are eternal.

That which is eternal still Remains up to this day, because it is not subjected to time.

For as Christ walks so shall we walk in the mind and the body of Christ; Exercising ourselves in one with the Holy Ghost who confirms that me and you together,In the spirit of God abide within us.

CHAPTER 6

(THE POWER OF THE WORD)

If we may operate in Authority by the Son and the Holy Ghost in us, Then everything a spiritual aspect of the Creator who created these things that which is experience for he is still here as in heaven,
as it is on Earth.
The spiritual things that was manifest and made visible, where the thing that was made by Him(THE CARPENTER). And for Him with Him,(those things made).
Anything that was not made by God. Not created of God,

CHAPTER 7

(IDOLS)

Is opposed against God these are the physical aspects of the carnal mind. Jesus said :

For us not to be conformed to the physical aspect of the carnal of THY eye that is intimate against God In Heaven

But be ye transformed by the renewing of Your Mind through Christ Jesus. walking after the mind of Christ.

For those carry the body of Christ (That's the perfection of the cross)

For those who partake Of The Body And The Blood Of The Truth Of Light of God.

Jesus was resurrected so that body that remains in us is the resurrected body of Jesus Christ.

(THE SUBSTANCE)

For it is the subatance of the spirit of the communion made flesh,

That He abides in us.(The Trinity Of God In Man) We live for Christ out of sight operate in the body of his body that dwells within our bellies .

That is the flesh and blood that we would take of the body of Christ which is the true body.

(You have not because you ask not)

(You have not because you ask not)

for the Lord will give to you those things that you ask.

I AM The Lord WHO WILL:

(THAT): there be spiritual strength of spiritual gifts,

these things we can ask the Lord for when we are in his purpose and his will to ask him for these things through the knowledge of the Holy Ghost WHOM speak what HE hears said,

And what HEAVEN says And the Holy Ghost shall speak.

And He will give you what you should speak in that very hour, then you speak those things back to God. (Walking in the spirit and not after the flesh):

As we walk in the flesh, but not after the flesh,

But we walk in the spirit for all things. That we see through the (eye) of the creator of spirit,

when the whole body is filled with the lights up the single eye,

When we are walking in the mind of Christ,

which is Spiritual for all things that are manifest was created in spirit,

that we will no longer are subjected to time, but to Eternity .

As we are one with Christ as He in the Father is one, so shall we be one with Jehovah the most high God.

Therefore, discerning the things around us in the spiritual aspect of His true creation, That is walking in the spirit. Discerning the two separate reality;

The reality of that of the conscious and carnal mind of the physical aspects.

And consciousness of the spirit of Christ by whom we walk in and walk After. where we meet up and came to know and to understand.

By using the five senses of that Flesh that was created that you're not (the flesh) going to Heaven, But we only return back to the ground which God called the body from.

The population in this world that we live in, for we walk out the faith night after night for thinking it's a site of the spiritual aspect of understanding. walking in the likeness of Christ in the spiritual understanding of the environment that we are in is certain places and things situations and circumstances is it up God to test them. (Testing the spirit by the holy spirit.)

(Testing the spirit by the holy spirit.)

to see whether they are of God or Not by the word of God written on your heart confirmed by the word of God that is written upon your the hidden man of your heart which is the heart of God in you.

CHAPTER 8

(A REVELATION)

A revelations from God and Even the understanding of the wisdom that he has given to me according to that which is not spoken.

Before the law what's the coming of the rapture according to the fleshly understanding of its own creation? According to his own understanding that is carnal-minded wisdom outside of God.

Inside that's the spiritual mind that is God's will.

For His will is SPIRITUAL,

One must be spiritual to commune with Him that is Spiritual.

FOR all things are spiritual, and what He spoke came from being invisible to visible from out of time (enternalty), and subjected in time, (physical).

And as the human body walks for those who know God and those who believe God and those who know there is a God, but understand nothing of the spiritual understanding of God.

(Those who are asleep)

(Those who are asleep) and do not know they sleeping those that are waking but they are asleep to walk in the physical aspect of understanding is in time will you communicate with the word of God and Christ abide in you communicate to his father that you are in spiritout of time communicating with the things out of time created by he that is out of time that is the same he him that created all things in time but they came out of time in and out in and out of time you have to walk your Earthly walk but are you more in time or out of time in your Earthly walk for how much out of time did you spend this day how much in time did you account for this day in and out in and out in and out the operator this day how much in and out in and out in and out in a twinkle of the eye they will be caught up in the rapture why those that was in time when miss the rapture for the Rapture is spiritual that is invisible for only those that have a spiritual eye with a spiritual understanding given to him by God can look at the things in the spirit the rapture for you you must know in time and out of time that's why he said pray and watch for when we pray for those who know how to pray to their father who are in here knows he their relationship with Christ they know when I'm praying in my room or in that cell will not desire is to reach out and to God tune out all the aspects of the physical existence of my life and isolate the body I put my heart why the body was in time that's so in the spirit of the body was communion with the father out of time out of time is an eternity in time is that that's injected out of Eternity into itself call time in and out in and out as we walk a spiritual walk with wisdom from God that we may understand the spiritual walk that he has for our life.

    Because he said don't never lean unto thy own understanding but by every word that proceedeth out of the mouth of GOD.

CHAPTER 9

LET NO MAN JUDGE YOU

How can one you say because you're sinning, that you cannot receive the word of God for the Bible says no man is perfect for all have sinned and fallen short of the glory of God The flesh doesn't want us to receive the word of God which I confirm it is the word of God while the flesh is in indulging, and seeing forget not his light shine in darkness that's what he said let your light shine after that one sheep that one sheep that has fell away from the flock but he loved his sheep, and I will fear no evil why because thou art with me so I will never leave you nor forsake you and God said let there be light and there were light and darkness cannot comprehend the lights how can we preach the word of God why the flesh is committing sin? For the flesh is shaped in iniquity in is born in sin,

For the flesh will always be sinful, that's why It cannot get into heaven. when Jesus went to the well and spoke to the Samaritan woman the Samaritan woman brought forth a truth a truth Jesus brought truth to her the Samaritan woman who is defiled in considered as a dog that that is unclean and when Jesus put the light in her and her light begin to shine she took the body of that that is unclean to the rest of those that are unclean and her light shine amongst those that were uncleanend those that were unclean came to Christ and all of them became clean God has dominion over all things even the flesh when he wants to operate according to the flesh for the flesh will always be in sin.

You cannot wash dirt from dirt and don't have dirt it's only because we are saved by Grace.

I let my light shine wherever I may go in the word itis being brought forth that may also save the soul, we War not

against flesh and blood but spirits and principalities in high places.
      Illuminated darkness that has captivated us and brought us into captivity but by the grace of the holy spirit in the word of God that covers Us that brings into us that Marvelous Light to overcome the darkness that we have walked in according to that of the flesh for the word has Dominion even over the things of the flesh that we may not be led and ignorant but by Deliverance by the grace of God in all wisdom knowledge and understanding even in the dark places of Our Lives. To overcome the darkness that we have walked in according to that of the flesh for the word has Dominion even over the things of the flesh that we may not be led and ignorant but by Deliverance by the grace of God in all wisdom knowledge and understanding actually the possession of the unclean spirit that it is connected to your body .dark places of Our Lives.

CHAPTER 10

UNDERSTANDING OF SIGHT

The word of God brings clarity to the understanding that what the mind is the understanding that the mind is hearing it's the words that those that are not spiritually-minded but as it hit your carnal mind for your carnal mind now lays dormant that's the spirit that is in you has taken dominion over the physical attributes of the body as a response.

A carnal mind is a mind that is intimate against the word of God that is a carnal mind.

THE DIVISION

The soul that became divided as a whole and then one that's with the soul for one part of the Soul gives a understanding the rationale of the spirit that's in you while the other part of the Soul rationale and receive the things on the outside of the shell which is the world to understand the the ways of man according to the physical understanding of your mind for your mind is shaped according to the conscience which gives you the weariness of I carnal is knowledge of seeing t that which is in the earth that is upon the Earth it gives you the knowledge of games that is against God for you have tasted the goodness of the Lord and the sourness of the devil and there is a difference but the one that you hold clean is that of the carnal mind which is the physical distractions that is giving it to you that gives the body a physical characteristic of the understanding that is bringing to you those are situations and circumstances, and all things that are negative and not of God that you have become emotionally attached to.

The understanding of the conscience which is the carnal mind for the carnal mind is intimate against the will of God, you cannot worship god with a carnal understanding a conscious. understanding is the understanding of the word of man with a conscious knowledge and wisdom of the world and not of God so you get the understanding of what man teach you and not the understanding as to what God has given to you.

CHAPTER 11

(Don't Believe Every Spirit)

Be not conformed to the eye of Darkness connecting to the eye of the spirit that dwells within you, but keep the eye of the light of the spirit that's the eye of God that is connected to you that you may see that i in you and you in me is the connection with your father;

(Know The light In You)

For your light is being shined upon the father as he's giving you light for The Spirit of God is the light of the body

(THE WILL)

Now spiritually minded is that free Will of Man which desire to do the do the will of God. That is the Breath of God that is put into this corrupt body that was born in iniquity and shaped in Sin; seeing that can never be perfect because it is seen the dirt of the earth which is corrupted even as Cain killed Abel and in this Blood spilled into the world.

So where we are we worship and become connected with the teachings in the love of God for you must love God and all that you love the word but you must love the word into and all that you connect with God for Jesus hence the word for another tool of the word that means you must love his Commandments for the word is keep my Commandments

(The Love)

If you love me for now our walk become righteous as we understand the Temptation that comes before us that gives us to the desires of the flesh.

The Familiarity of the iniquity that has given birth to at once more and now remembers,

Bringing back the remembrance of the things that God has done away with and has forgotten, that you may come back to remember and go back and Resurrect The Dead.

TO resurrect the dead are the sins that God cast into the sea of forgiveness and never to remember no more only for you to go into the graveyard and dig up the sin and bring that back into a resurrection into your life.

CHAPTER 12

(LET THE DEAD BURY THE DEAD)

Having to go back to God to get rid of the thing that you have resurrected upon yourself because you looked away from God and your eyes connect to the eye of darkness which is that that conforms you to the world that gives them carnal mind dominion over the flesh to give carnal thing.

(Don't look Back)
To look back as lot wife look back at Solomon Gomorrah as God forgave them leaving sodom and Gomorrah the sins of Sodom and Gomorrah and she looks back at the things that God forgave her for and she resurrected the sins God forgave her for, but yet conform to those things she desired and turned into a pillar of salt resurrecting the sins that she was forgiven

(What's for me is for me)
Only when I get a revelation from God if I see visions the revelations from God anything's God given to me even hide the understanding that he has given to me.

Having to go back to God to get rid of the thing that you have resurrected upon yourself because you looked away from God and your eyes we can't connect it to the eye of darkness which is that that conforms you to the world that gives them carnal mind dominion over the flesh to give carnal thing.

That is carnal minded which is against the kingdom of God.

But where you are to dealing with God and you going to the house that the Holy Ghost is dwelling within us;

Because this is a house that the Lord has blessed a house that has much righteousness and faith that the Holy

Ghost will dwells amongs those that coming to the collect the body.

As one body As one body to become subject to under the spirit that has become one and spirit in one mine to go into the house of the Lord that they made themselves and to the Holy Ghost Church those that believe and understand the faith and walk into the faith and know and believe that Jesus died on the cross for my sins obeying the Commandments in the teachings of the book that we may believe with an understanding that the word of God may give us a Divine understanding but when we seek the word understanding of seek ye first the kingdom of God is wisdom only the wise would not guilty to the word of God that Prosperity maybe spiritual as well as physically move and letting God moves in our life when we get out the way of our own conscious mind for our conscious mind keep us in a Consciousness that is intimate against the spirit of God and our Lord Christ Jesus

CHAPTER 13

(Knowing The Difference)

Because the conscience is that the gives you awareness the wellness but the carnal mind is those things that give you the dark spiritual attributes of the physical conscious.

Understand that you will always be distracted about the things that you are able to see and never understand the spiritual demons that have built the things that you was designed to see.

You want to know why I record now you see why.

let me ask you a question.

Did you to recognize Jesus in the knowledge that is given to you?

How many preachers must first go into the scriptures that they make as mold-hills and shape the people mind that they never see the Mountains of the word may say what Jesus has done that they mine may be conformed to the image of Jesus with that understanding but you Jesus is

in all good things for only he is good.

Book One: The Breath of God In Us

BOOK TWO
REVISED

THE
TRINITY OF GOD
IN MAN
BY
ANTHONY WALKER

Earthly Stories with a Heavenly Meaning

Anthony Walker

Book Two
Revised

The
Trinity of God
in Man
By
Anthony Walker

PUBLISHED by PARABLES
Earthly Stories with a Heavenly Meaning

Anthony Walker

Book 1: The Breath of God In Us
Book 2: The Trinity OF God In Man
Anthony Walker

Published By Parables
May, 2020

All Rights Reserved. No part of this book may be reproduced or utilized in any form or by any means, electronic or mechanical, including photocopying, recording, or by any information storage and retrieval system, without permission in writing from the author.

    Printed in the United States of America

Readers should be aware that Internet Web sites offered as citations and/or sources for further information may have been changed or disappeared between the time this was written and the time it is read.

Book Two: The Trinity Of God In Man

In the beginning was the Word,
and the Word was with God,
and the Word was God.

    To read something and to hear something spoken bring two different understandings, by the way that it has been administered into the body, which is the mind and the soul. The mind is carnal, governing the external existence of man, who walks in the course of time intimate against God, only receiving understanding from the "prince of the power of the air," which is Satan, who governs the air of the earth that was given over to him by the fall of man. Internally, there is the wisdom and knowledge given to us by the Divine. What is carnal and what is spiritual are in intimate darkness, and that which is the true light of God.

CHAPTER 1

To understand the physical aspects of understanding, we must first understand spiritual aspects of understanding, which comes from the divine revelation of God, given unto us who abide in Christ, that in all things the Spirit of the Holy Ghost, by Christ which is given to him by his Father who gives it unto the Holy Ghost – amen! – that will quicken our Spirit of the revelation of the mind of Christ unto the mind and wisdom of God. For our battles are not of flesh and blood, but of spirits and principalities, for all things were created first in the Spirit. Should we not be concerned also by these things of the carnal – first created in the Spirit by the Spirit – that all things are Spirit as we walk spiritually in the mind of Christ? We are fighting against these things that are carnal, operating through the carnal, manifesting themselves from what's invisible made visible over the free will of man – TO WHOM YOU WILL YOUR MEMBERS, TO WHOM YOU WILL SERVE – according to the desire of man, whether the Spirit of God who leads man to righteousness according to the desire of his heart, or the devil who tempts.

A man, by the desire of his own wicked flesh and his own wicked imagination, comes against the Word of God. For Christ asked, "In the physical aspects of understanding, who do they say I am?" and Peter said, "In the physical aspect of understanding, they say that you were John the Baptist, you are that prophet." A Jesus asked, "Who do you say I am?" And Peter answered according to the spiritual aspect of understanding – for we walk after the Spirit and not by sight – "You are the Christ, the only begotten Son of the most high God, who sits on the right hand of the Father."

What will not conform to the things of this world, the physical aspects of these things, will be transformed by the renewal of our minds with Christ. We walk after the Spirit, not after the flesh, seeing all things that are whole and true. They are the truth, first in the spirit, manifested in the flesh. That we manifest things that are in the flesh, do those things that are in the Spirit – whether person, places, or things, situations, or circumstance – before we decide those things of the Spirit to see whether these spirits be of God are not by the spirit; in the world with your spirit, by the spirit. In all things, remain spiritual, not of the flesh; but those things that are of the light, for the darkness comprehended light not. We war not against flesh and blood, but spiritual principalities.

For the light of the body is the eye. We see those things of spiritual understanding through the mind of Christ, whom we know and who we are. Therefore, when the eye is single, we are of one mind with Christ, as he is the head of his temple where even we as his children abide in him, that whatever a man thinketh so is he. Are we not also as he thinketh, that our whole body also is full of light? But those who are not in Christ, their eye is evil, and the darkness comprehends the light not, and many see and see not, understand but understand not, and the darkness becomes an imitation of that light, and they are drawn to that light because they are not of the light.

"Then you will know the truth, and the truth will set you free." John 8:32

He spoke these words, and many believed in him. Then said Jesus to those Jews who believed in him, "if you continue in my Word, then you are my disciples, and you shall know the truth, and the truth shall make you free." To believe the physical aspect of Jesus is the faith to come to know the spiritual aspect that you believe in, which is Christ. When I began my walk with the Lord, I knew nothing other than that he that was crucified and rose for my salvation, which I understood according to the teaching that I believed, but yet had not come to know him in whom I first believed.

CHAPTER 2

Born in Sin

I was born July 11, 1972, to my parents, Ethel Walker and Lester Walker. I have two brothers and a sister, and we grew up in the church. Our household was a believer of Christ. We went to church regularly; my whole family is mostly teachers and ministers, coming from the bloodline of the Bradley family for Monroeville, Alabama. My great uncle Curtis is a patriarch, a pastor's pastor: he is the head.

The best way I can sum this up is to tell you how I receive my calling. I was just normal, like everybody else. My birth was kind of strange, yet I was still normal and I grew up in the church. We believed those who knew Christ, but only told us to believe in Jesus, for you have to know him for yourself. Those who abide in Christ, who come to know Christ first, believe in Jesus, even God who sent him, who drew you into the Lord. No man can commit to the Lord unless God sends him, and no man can be drawn into me unless he is given to me by the Father, who sends me. He is drawn in, who is the son of man. For this is my flesh, and this is my blood, bone of my bone, marrow of my love for you and him.

Are we made perfect for Christ? He died to repent of all things that have been chosen to burden us, but yet he died for us, that he could pardon all sins, so that we owe nothing to the world. For he said, "no man but him has purchased you for a precious price, and that is Christ."

I have not always talked this way. I knew Christ, but one day the Lord delivered me from the evil of temptation. He did not leave me, but I was drawn into this temptation by my own lustful desires, even the devices which are unclean spirits. In seeing the error of my life – the addiction, the whoremongering and spirits – these things I've come to know now, through the understanding. I was ignorant when I was walking into that understanding, but he delivered me from the evils of temptation. I was caught in a trap, in the snare, and I knew this evil that I did before God. I was able to call out to him, so that he could relieve me from this selfishness, this foolishness that I did.

And God moved me, for the first time that I remember. I was caught up in despair, crying so much before God, for this evil that I did. I knew it was wrong, and I called out and asked, "God, if you remove this from my life, I will follow you forever." And behold, after three days, it disappeared – and I never saw it again. I knew then that the Lord called me.

I asked the Lord for wisdom and knowledge and understanding, and then I began to search. I grew up in church with the knowledge of who God is to those that called us, but I knew I had to go deeper: I had to know Christ.

I started searching for his face in the scripture, and as I began to search, I began to pray. It began to open up to me, and in that moment of the scripture opening up to me, I began to see revelation. I began to pray the prayers as Jesus said to pray these prayers – don't just listen, but behold what he says, not as a figure of speech but as it is. I began to ask God for the understanding of the Word of God, to increase in the Word of God, to be a mighty man in the

Word of God, to be pleasing in his eyes, that he ordain this one as a mighty man of God.

I said it to the Lord, "whatever I have to do, whatever you have to do, to make me to be the man you want me to be, I will pick that cross up and carry it." I may complain, I may backslide, I may do all these things along the way, but I will still carry that cross and be faithful to that Word because I know the promises of God that abide in me. I have seen in the land of the living, the blessing that he has restored in my life.

As I was looking at this blessing in my life – which shall come to pass for his Word is true – as I began to go on these journeys with the Lord, I consulted him. In all these things that I went through, it was the Word of God, the Word of the Spirit in the Lord, that told us that when you see the rain, come together. That is the fulfillment of the Word that you see, the revelation, the parable of that Word for you.

If you see the power, then you see the truth. Did you see the physical aspect of that which is spiritual, that which is physical? You see the rightly divine Word in the truth of all truth; you see the creation that has been made from nothing. Show me the secrets in the mysteries of the scriptures, and the Lord who says, "If you go before my Father and ask my Father anything in my name, my Father will give it to you. If you ask me anything in my name, I will give it to you." And I said unto the Lord, "I do want to come into thy name, but he that abides in me is also advising me." Those that come to know, also become one with the Father, for you and me, and me and you, for me and my father are one. For who do they say that I am? I am that I am.

CHAPTER 3

The Bio

As I'm writing this book, the Lord touches me. When the Lord touches me, he begins to speak. You have to have a clean vessel; the bowl with oil of the Word will overflow, for he says, "my cup runneth over." Do you really understand the 23rd psalm? "For the Lord is my shepherd," reminds me that I'm about to give in to this, seeing that he's not going to leave me astray from the flock. The Lord is my shepherd! I know this because I've given over to my own self and my own lustful desires, which are still in the corner of my mind. I lean into my own understanding, which is separate from the flock. I may be only one, but the Lord is my shepherd: I shall not want.

What aspect of your life is that that you "shall not want?" Do we consider the words of God when we repeat and rehearse and recite the Word of God? Or do we speak these elements that are the substance of faith? A word that you cannot see – and the evidence of the things hopeful – is the first base of belief. Everything else is doubt!

"He makes me lie down in green pastures" – understand that I started off on this journey down this road, this scene with my shepherd in mind. I'm taking him with me, for the Lord is my shepherd. I know I'm going to go – I hope I can make it back. For I shall not want, for I know that the Good Shepherd will come find me if I'm gone too long. He leads me in the path of righteousness, for his namesake is the reason I recognize the evil of things, when I'm wondering about the difference to know the truth. He leads me in the paths of righteousness for his namesake. Yea, though I walk through the valley of shadow of death, I will fear no evil; for I know I'm covered, and I'm anointed.

I know that tomorrow is short for me, for what he has for me has not come to pass, but I wear his promise until the end. I am sure that I will be there tomorrow. There are things that I do in my foolishness, but the wisdom of God walks upon the earth. For we are the children of Christ, even in the dark place, the valley of the shadow of death. That power is of the dark, hiding his treasures in dark places, but those that walk in the light – for what is in the dark shall be revealed to that light – will behold what was hidden.

Even in the dark place, all things that belong to God are good. Why do you seek those that are in the dark with the evil gods? That dark place is foolishness, but look to the wisdom and Word of God. We ask God to elevate us, for the Lord says many will come to the door, but only a few dine therein, for some see not, and understand not, and hear not.

"Think not that I am come to destroy the law, or the prophets: I am not come to destroy, but to fulfill." (Matthew 5:17) Know that you may understand the whole truth, that one truth bears witness. In him is the truth, for he is the truth that leads us into all truth. Even those that are forsaken confess he is the truth. They confess their sins, for those are true.

We ask the Lord to lead us not into temptation, but to deliver us from the evil of the temptation that we know not. If I follow the crooked path of temptation, I pray that it may be made straight, so that I'm delivered from the evil of that temptation.

The Lord said, "Any man that comes before me, and asks the Father for anything in my name, I will give it, for my Father and I are one. Who could come unto the Father except through the Son?" This means that Father and Son are one. You abide also in the Father, for you are one with him, as I am one with the Father also: "I am the way, the truth, and the life: no man cometh unto the Father, but by me." (John 14:6)

God has given me the understanding to become one mind, one soul, one body, one church, one faith, one God, one Father, all united in the name of Jesus Christ. We come unto him, we hear him, for he reveals himself to be in the name of Jesus. I thank you Father in the name of Jesus Christ. Those that awaken must be also of God in the understanding of what they see, for some see not; but they are called to a higher calling into the mount of transfiguration by the Holy Spirit. We see all things in the truth, for both of us are him, and he is us. We are one in Christ!

Yes, we are glory! Glory to the Lord, who has been there to give us this divine revelation and knowledge. We judge not that we may not be judged, but judge those things which can only be seen in the spirit, which manifests those things that are not seen – by those that can only see with both eyes. He has sent me, me and not him – and him and me –to receive his divine understanding, even administering of the tongues in the evening –angelic songs and diverse types of songs, even those in diverse tongues.

I ask you for Jesus, walking in revelation in the Word of God. What we speak is what is so, for we see what we speak. What we speak is what we saw, by him who created what we saw in Heaven, as it is on earth for our body. He and I, together we go before. Ask our Father who is in heaven, in my name, for giving to me in heaven, as I give to him on Earth. All that he asked for is granted, that he may receive, as I do; what is given to him, that was given to you.

CHAPTER 4

The Manifestation of the Promise of Prayer

In my distress I called on the Lord, and I cried to my God. He heard my voice out of his temple; my cry came to his ears.

The Lord looked down from heaven upon the children of men, even unto me, to see if there were any who seek God.

Any man that lacks wisdom, let him ask of the Father, Who gives in abundance. Teach me to pray – for I know not what others pray for – according to the spiritual wisdom and knowledge that surpass all understanding.

I asked the Lord that I may know wisdom, and receive the word of understanding. To receive the instruction of wisdom, righteousness, judgment, and equality; to give prudence to simple knowledge; to convey all this to the young, to understand a proverb and its interpretation, and the words of the wise – this is the wisdom with which the Lord has blessed me.

I ask the Lord for the wisdom to understand the error of my ways, to cleanse me of my secret faults. I kept back His servant also from presumptuous sins. Do not let them rule over me! I shall be blameless, innocent of great transgressions. Let the words of my mouth and the meditation of my heart be acceptable in Your sight, oh Lord, my rock and my redeemer!

Your Word has been tried and proven faithful. If any man lack wisdom in these things, let him ask of the Father concerning them. He will give you an abundance of unbridled wisdom. If you lack in these things, then you lack wisdom.

The law of the Lord is perfect. Restoring to the soul, the testimony of the Lord is makes the simple wise. The precepts of the Lord are right, rejoicing the heart. The commandments of the Lord are pure enlightenment to the eyes.

The fear of the Lord is endures forever; the judgment of the Lord is altogether true and righteous. More to be desired than gold – yes, much finer than gold, sweeter also – is the honey in the honeycomb that is the substance of the things in heaven. What I desire is the love of God that surpasses all understanding, that brings forth a peace that surpasses all understanding in heaven, that surpasses all things that are on Earth.

And these things I asked of you, and other things I asked of the Lord, that I may walk in holiness and righteousness; that we may become the image of the son, God that was created first in their image in the first creation of the manifestation of the image of God the Son, the Father, and the Holy Spirit made flesh in heaven as it is on Earth.

CHAPTER 5

The Supplication of Prayer

"If any of you lack wisdom, let him ask of God, that giveth to all men liberally, and upbraideth not; and it shall be given him." (James 1:5)

For if any man asks me anything in my name, to be one with him and His name, I would give it to you. I ask God that I be the blessed man who does not walk in the counsel of the wicked nor stand in the way of sinners, nor sit in the seat of the scornful, but his delight is in the law of the Lord. Now that my delight is the law of the Lord, in your law do I meditate day and night. I shall be like a tree planted by the stream of water that brings forth its fruit in season, and whose leaf does not wither. In all that I do, I shall prosper!

The wicked are like a breath which the wind rises away, therefore the wicked should not stand in the judgment, nor sinners in the congregation of the righteous; for the Lord knows the way of the righteous, but the way of the wicked shall perish. In my distress, I called on the Lord, and I cried to my God, and he heard my voice out of His Temple. As my cry came before him into His ears, the Lord looked down from heaven upon the children of man, even myself, to see if there were any who understand and who seek after God.

O Lord, I pray to you according to all Your righteousness. Let Your anger and Your fury be turned away from Your city, Jerusalem, Your holy mountain. Because of our sins – even my sins – the iniquities of our fault are generational curses. Jerusalem and Your people have become a reproach to all those who are around us. And now O God, hear the prayer of Your servant and his supplication, and cause Your face to shine upon Your sanctuary that is desolate, for the Lord's sake. O my God, incline Your ear and hear, open Your eyes and behold: our destination is the city, which is called by Your name. We do not present our supplications before you on account of our righteousness, but because of Your great mercies. O Lord, hear! O Lord, forgive! O lord, hurry and do not delay for Your own sake. O my God, Your city and Your people are called by Your name.

While I was speaking and praying and confessing my sins and the sins of my people, Israel, and presenting my supplication before the Lord my God, for the Holy mountain of my God; yea while I was speaking in prayer, even the man Gabriel who I have seen in the bedroom at the beginning, being caused to fly swiftly, came to me, about the time of the evening sacrifice.

And he made me understand, and talked with me, and said, "O Anthony, as he also said unto Daniel, I have now come forth to give you insight and understand at the beginning of your supplication. For the Word says, 'confess your sins one to another even unto God.' The Word went forth and I have come, for you are greatly beloved; therefore consider the Word and understand the vision.

CHAPTER 6

A revelation from God Beyond thought: understanding the wisdom that he has given to me, not only speaking what is beautiful. As you heard the Word of God, it reminded you of a poem, and at the end you said, "I want to listen to the end." It says, "I love you in and out of time – in and out, in and out, in and out. I told you that some poems have to be inspired, remember? This is what I saw before the law, the coming of the rapture, free according to the fleshly understanding of its own creation, according to his own understanding, which is carnal-minded wisdom outside of God.

Inside is the spiritual mind that is God's will. For his will is spiritual; one must be spiritual to commune with him who is spiritual, for all things are spiritual. What he spoke went from being invisible, to being revealed from out of time (eternity), and subjected to time (physical). The human body wakes for those who know God, and those who believe God, and those who know there is a God, but understand nothing of the spiritual understanding of God.

Those who are asleep and do not know they are sleeping, those that are waking, but are asleep too, walk in the physical aspect of understanding. In time, you will communicate with the Word of God, and Christ will abide in you and communicate to His Father that you are in Spirit out of time, communicating with the things out of time created by him who is out of time. The same one that created all things in time, yet they came out of time – in and out, in and out of time.

You have to walk your earthly walk, but are you more in time, or out of time in your earthly walk? How much out of time did you spend this day? How much in time did you account for this day – in and out, in and out, in and out. How much in and out – in and out, in and out? In a twinkle of the eye, they will be caught up in the Rapture, while those that were in time then miss the Rapture. For the Rapture is spiritual, visible only to those who have a spiritual understanding given to them by God. They can look at the things in the spirit, the Rapture. You must know that in time, and out of time – that is why he said, "pray and watch, for when we pray for those who know how to pray to their Father Who is here, knows he their relationship with Christ."

When I'm praying in my room or in the cell, I desire is to reach out to God, to tune out all the aspects of the physical existence of my life and isolate the body. I put my heart where the body was in time, so in the Spirit of the body is communion with the Father out of time. Out-of-time is an eternity in time, is ejected out of eternity into itself.

Call time – in and out, in and out – as we walk a spiritual walk with wisdom from God, that we may understand the spiritual walk that he has for our life. He said, "don't ever lean unto thine own understanding, but by every word that proceedeth out of the mouth of God."

How can you say that because you're sinning, that you cannot receive the Word of God? As you just said: it is the WORD OF GOD. You said, "well, why doesn't the flesh want us to receive the Word of God?" I confirm that it is the Word of God, while the flesh is indulgent, and seeing this, forget not His light that shines in darkness. That's what he said: "let your light shine after that one sheep that has fallen away from the flock."

He loved his sheep, and I will fear no evil. Why? Because thou art with me, so I will never leave you nor forsake you. God said, "let there be light," and there was light; and darkness cannot comprehend the light. How can we preach the Word of God while the flesh is committing sin? For the flesh is shaped in iniquity and is born in sin. The flesh will always be sinful; that's why It cannot get into heaven. When Jesus went to the well and spoke to the Samaritan woman, the Samaritan woman brought forth a truth – a truth Jesus had brought to her. The Samaritan woman, who is defiled and considered as a dog that that is unclean – when Jesus put the light in her, and her light begin to shine, she took the body of what is unclean to the those who are unclean. As her light shone amongst those that were unclean, they came to Christ, and all of thembecame clean.

God has dominion over all things, even the flesh. If you operate according to the flesh, the flesh will always be in sin. You cannot wash dirt from dirt. If we don't have dirt, it is only because we are saved by Grace.

I am blessed wherever I may go. The Word is being brought forth so that it may save the soul. We war not against flesh and blood, but spirits and principalities. Are you praying – are you prayed up? Because you are one who truly believes, exercise the power that has been given to you, that your life makes you better. Prosper for the sake of your children!

Getting high is a demon – the lowest self is actually the possession of the unclean spirit, connected to your body: that phrase, "I was not myself." What you see as a high is not a high, but is a distortion. It is illuminated darkness that captivates us and brings us into captivity. By the Grace of the Holy Spirit in the Word of God that covers us, that brings us into that marvelous light – THAT IS SPIRITUALLY MINDED – overcomes the darkness that we have walked in according to the flesh. For the Word has dominion, even over the things of the flesh, that we may not be led in ignorance, but by deliverance by the grace of God in all wisdom knowledge and understanding, even in the dark places of our lives.

Even now as you started to listen, the things that you received seem to fade away, for you no longer pay attention to the things that you were before, because you begin to see the things that you are hearing.

The omnipotent One brings you understanding. What you see brings clarity to the understanding that the mind is hearing life. They are the same words that those who are not spiritually minded hear too, but as they hit your carnal mind, your carnal mind now lies dormant. The Spirit that is in you has taken dominion over the physical attributes of the body.

What is a carnal mind? It is a mind that is intimate against the Word of God. The carnal mind is part of a soul that has become divided. One part of the soul gives an understanding of the Spirit that's in you, while the other part of the soul receives the things on the outside of the shell, which is the world. Understand the ways of man according to the physical understanding of your mind, for your mind is shaped according to the conscience, which gives you the weariness of carnality. Carnal is the sight, the knowledge of seeing what is upon the Earth. It gives you the knowledge of games, which are against God. You have tasted the goodness of the Lord and the sourness of the devil, and there is a difference – but the one that you hold is that of the carnal mind. It is the physical distraction that gives it to you, that gives the body a physical characteristic of the understanding of what brings you those situations and circumstances.

You have become emotionally attached to things that are negative and not of God. This is the understanding of the conscience, which is the carnal mind, for the carnal mind is intimate against the will of God. You cannot worship God with a carnal understanding.

A conscious understanding is the understanding of the word of man, with a conscious knowledge of the world that is not of God. You understand only what man teaches you, and not what God has given to you. The body is manipulated to hide away from the eye of God. He has connected his Self with the eye of darkness. Be not conformed to the eye of darkness; connect with the eye of the Spirit that dwells within you, but keep the eye of the Spirit that dwells in you, the eye of God that is connected to you, that you may see eye for eye. Eye-for-eye is a connection with your Father, for your life is being shone upon the Father as he's giving you light.

CHAPTER 7

The Spirit of God is the light of the body. The free will of man is spiritually minded, with a desire to do the word and the will of God. The breath of God is put into this corrupt body that was born in iniquity and shaped, that can never be perfect because it has seen the dirt of the earth, which is corrupted. Even as Cain killed Abel, this blood spilled into the soil where we worship and become connected with the teachings in the love of God. You must love God, but you must also love the Word to connect with God. This means you must love his commandments. "Keep my commandments if you love me," – now I will become righteous, as we understand the temptation that comes before us, that gives us to the desires of the flesh.

The familiarity of iniquity has given birth once more, and now brings back the remembrance of the things that God has done away with, that you may come back to remember and resurrect the dead. God cast your sins into the sea of forgiveness, never to be remembered anymore, only for you to go into the graveyard and dig them up, bringing them back like a resurrection into your life. You have to go back to God to get rid of the sins that you have resurrected upon yourself, because you looked away from God and your eyes were connected to the eye of darkness. This makes you conform to the world, giving the carnal mind dominion over the flesh, giving in to the carnal thing.

Do not look back as Lot's wife looked back at Sodom and Gomorrah. God forgave them, leaving the sins of Sodom and Gomorrah behind, yet she looked back at the things that God forgave her for, and she resurrected the forgiven sins. She conformed to those things she desired, and in turning against the Kingdom of God, she turned into a pillar of salt.

When you deal with God, you go into the house where the Holy Ghost dwells. This is a house that the Lord has blessed, a house that has much righteousness and faith. The Holy Ghost will dwell among those that come together as one body under the Spirit, as one Spirit and one mind, to go into the house of the Lord that they made themselves, and to the Holy Ghost Church. They believe and understand the faith, walking in the faith, knowing and believing that Jesus died on the cross for our sins, obeying the commandments in the teachings of the Book. We believe that the Word of God gives us a divine understanding. "Seek ye first the Kingdom of God," is wisdom for the wise. Prosperity may be spiritual as well as physical, letting God move in our lives. We must get out the way of our own conscious mind that keeps us in a consciousness that is intimate against the Spirit of God and our Lord Christ Jesus.

Conscience brings awareness, but the carnal mind encompasses those things that endow dark spiritual attributes with physical consciousness. You will always be distracted by the things that you are able to see, never understanding the spiritual demons that have built the things that you were designed to see.

You want to know why I write? Now you see why. Let me ask you a question, get you to recognize Jesus in the knowledge that is given to you: how many preachers must first go into the scriptures so that they can make, mold, and shape people's minds, that they may say what Jesus has done, that their minds may be conformed to the image of Jesus? Jesus is in all good things, for only he is good.

CHAPTER 8

Explaining a Mindset

I do not think myself so complicated, nor do I consider myself to be higher than anyone, by the wisdom of God who gives me an understanding of how to humble myself. I don't pretend to know why I'm in the Lord, yet not comfortable in the Lord. People can judge only what they see, and understand only according to their understanding. You could understand by your own understanding, or ask God, who surpasses your own understanding. Compassionate and understanding is the prophet from God!

Growing up, even my birth was a topic of conversation. My mama was with Jesus – her life ceased as I came out of her womb, and it's always been the most fascinating story I have ever heard. In all the stories I've heard on this matter, from three women, the substances had no effect on where I am, only where the body appears to be. "How to separate an egg?" so I said. Let man judge how they judge and understand according to their understanding.

These are the type of things for which I give glory to God, for we are born out of the flesh and of the Spirit. How then to choose? A love of Christ must be taught. We must learn how to walk and become one with Christ, but no one can be plucked out of his hand, not even me or you

CHAPTER 9

Christ and His Prophets

The truth or fiction of a prophet is rightly seen when we read 2 Corinthians 10. He says, "How do I know, according to the understanding in the will of God, if the preacher has not preached it? How does a preacher preach, if he's not sitting by God with the gifts of revelation of what is about to go forth in the name of Jesus?" (2 Corinthians 10)

The apostles give a measurement of gifts, first reminding us of the weapons of our warfare. It's not people, places, things, situations, or circumstances that are manifested. Tangible things manifest over time, but our war is spiritual. The workers of iniquity build up things that become tangible.

The young prophet was telling me, "and behold, the Word of God tells me in 2 Corinthians 10:7, "Do ye look on things after the outward appearance? If any man trust to himself that he is Christ's, let him think again that, as he is Christ's, even so are we Christ's." We who abide in Christ but don't look at the outer appearance of a thing, seeing it from the inner appearance of our well-being verses the letter of the Word, what we are asking? That will be also when we present how to hide you from your own flesh, so you're blinding me from me.

CHAPTER 10

A Look into the Mind of a Prophet

Heavenly Father, we come to your holy throne of grace in the name of Jesus. You say that when we are gathered in your name, that you are in our midst. Lord God, thank you this morning for another beautiful blessed day in the name of Jesus. Thank you for giving us the right mindset this morning. Lord, thank you for covering us while we slept. In the name of Jesus, Father, petition and supplication to you, Father. Eyes open, Lord God. In the name of Jesus, because you said in your Word, Lord, not to live by bread alone, but by every word that proceeds from the mouth of God and falls. Thank you for overflowing us with your Word. Come and get any of the vileness – voodoo, witchcraft, Hinduism, anything that is contrary to your Word. Lord God, we come against this in the mighty name of Jesus.

The Father has many mansions for us, and we praise and give you the honor and glory. Lord God, we pray for protection over our children. We thank you for giving us a broken and contrite heart. We thank you, Lord, that you shed the skin of the unrighteous from us, and that you drove us back to you. I thank you for the chastening of God. I thank you for being able to come back and repent to you. I ask that you change us from our wicked ways, so that we stand in the whole righteously with you, Father. You are King of Kings, Lord of Lords.

CHAPTER 11

Lord God, we pray for the nations; we pray for the cities. We pray for the pastor and the church. We pray for everyone. You said that we are to go out and preach the good news. You said that you were with us, baptized in the Father, and the Son, and the Holy Spirit, and that you will be with us always until the very end of ages. We thank you for the wisdom and the knowledge and understanding, Lord. My hands are open to receive thy promise, now, FATHER, bless me to accept that which is received. AMEN

A Prayer to the Throne of Mercy

Oh heavenly gracious Father, teach us to pray, for we know not what we ought to pray for according to Your spiritual richness and understanding. With tender mercy, give us the understanding that surpasses all understanding, that we would lean not unto our own understanding of having a Father. You said that if any man lack wisdom, let him go to the Father, who gives in abundance. We are coming to your heavenly Father through the Spirit of the Holy Ghost. Give us this day, this very moment.

The Lord has blessed me, for his hand is upon my life. I could see the presence of the Lord in the life that I walked, which has been adorned by God from the beginning to the end. My life has begun: from the beginning to the end, I see all things that were created. As we walk from the beginning to the end, open the spirit. Paul says, "And lest I should be exalted above measure through the abundance of the revelations, there was given to me a thorn in the flesh, the messenger of Satan to buffet me, lest I should be exalted above measure. For this thing I besought the Lord thrice, that it might depart from me." (2 Corinthians 12:7–9)

    I call out in the name of Christ – as we become one with Christ – for Christ is abiding in us. We walk after the Spirit of Christ, walking after the spirit, not after the flesh. Yet we use the flesh to walk after the spirit. It is the spiritual made physical, for all that are called to a higher calling.

    Those are all children of Christ, who exercise the authority of Christ, for we are chosen. We are vessels of Christ: to be one with God is to be one with Christ, for he is one. We will be one with the Father. Paul says that he received the vine revelation and knowledge that were given to him. He is delivered from his reflections, not partaking in those things of the flesh. Those who abide in Christ, in the mind of Christ, will become one with Christ. He delivers us from our affliction in our souls as the Spirit comes into one mind.

    The Father shields us with the Son, that we do not partake in the things of the flesh. The flesh finds pleasure in the things of darkness, not comprehending the light. Wars rage against the spirit, against your mind of Christ, to whom you belong and whose vessel you are. The Spirit controls the mind of that vessel, whether it is carnal or spiritual. The carnal mind is led by the physical aspects of existence, which we call life. It is the physical aspect of the creation, by the spiritual aspect of the Creator of these things. You see according to what you understand. Do you see those things of the world, or do you see through the eyes of Christ? All things are spiritual.

I pray to the Lord to teach me to pray for I know not what to pray for according to your righteousness and your namesake. I speak the name of Jesus and pray for those that are in Christ. We walk after the spirit, not after the flesh, becoming one with Christ. I abide in you, and you in me. Where my Father is, so should I be, with you as we become one with the Father. Make your request known unto him, for any man that goes before my Father in my name and asks, with no doubt, it shall be given unto him.

We walk after the mind of Christ, for we are the children of Christ that abide in him. We are his sheep; we know his voice, turn towards his voice, his Word. We behold that voice, and see what is called revelation.

We hear the speech of those things that are spoken by the Spirit. We see those things that are created by the Spirit, not to be covered. All of those things are created by the Spirit. To abide in Christ is to walk after Christ, to know the speech and to speak it.

You are the one in the mind of Christ! Do you not understand my speech? What's invisible is made visible, for we walk not after the flesh, but after the Spirit. Lord, teach me to pray, for I know not what to pray. Go before me and make the crooked places straight. Forgive me of my misdeeds, Father, as I forgive everything by the blood of Christ, who overcame death and brought eternal life.

What old things have passed away! Behold, all things are made new in this eternal life. What is above the sun is new; all things under the sun, he passed away for. There is nothing new under the sun, but above the sun, "all things I do."

How can you cast a demon out of a person if you cannot see the demon that afflicts him? Yet we judge the affliction without casting out the demon afflicting that person. How do you call yourself of the faith, if you can't see by faith?

For we walk by faith, not by sight. Some are called to a higher calling, as even the apostles were: Peter, John, and James. As they were called into a higher calling, they saw the Father. They heard the Father; they even heard the Father speak to the Son. They listened to him, learning what is of Christ who abides in us, and us in him. But they said, "How do you see the spiritual aspect of understanding? For he draws all men unto him, those that were called to him by the Father, sent to us by him. When we walk in the spiritual aspect of understanding, we see differently; we hear differently."

You can cast the demon out of a person if you can see the demon that afflicts him. We focus not only on the affliction, but on the demon. How do you call yourself a seer if you can't see the spiritual aspect of understanding? As we walk after the mind of Christ, should we not also see the mind of Christ? All things are spiritual: Christ is spiritual, but he walked among man in the body of a perfect man. In Jesus dwelled a perfect being, a beloved man named Christ, who sits on the right-hand of the Father.

How can we say that we are watchers if we can't see the spiritual aspect of spiritual things? A spirit was created in the flesh; I was created in the flesh. You call yourselves watchers and overseers, but you cannot see that demon that walks in the church, because you call her Sister Patty. Your brothers and sisters cannot see those things, but yet you call yourself a pastor. You call on Brother John, but you don't see his affliction yourself.

The Spirit prays for me and sees the prayers made for me. When the Spirit prays for me, the Lord says, "you moved to lift him up." you cannot pull him up by showing his faults; you pull him up by lifting him. This is how you speak to him: build him up and he will see his own faults. Do not point out his faults while trying to raise him up.

This is the Word of God; it came to me because I asked him, that I may know how to talk to you. The Spirit is in the atmosphere; the shadow of his wings covers me in the Holy tabernacle of God. He is my refuge and my keeper.

The Lord has blessed me to see a great shifting, in time and in season. He moves through this season in this time, in the form of a tornado. He tears down those things that are not rooted, and disarranges the things that have been arranged by other hands. He tears down those things that were not by his hand, those that mimic and mock.

All things were made in the manifestation of the Word of God, and those things that were made by him are good. Be quick to hear and slow to speak. Be slow to anger, for the tribes of your patience increase your faith. Patience leads to perfect works. Be quick to hear and slow to speak, slow to anger and slow to show wrath. Let patience bring perfect works, that you may not be quick to anger nor quick to speak, but quick to hear.

You have to be in alignment with God to receive his gifts. They come with the acceptance that you received the instructions, the wisdom, knowledge, and understanding of the gift that you are being given. The Word of God and the acceptance of this gift from God will come.

We come to know Christ as he reveals himself through his body. The Word is of God, who is greater than those in the body of this vessel, who bring the Word to me, as a servant of God. The Word bears witness, for it is the Word of God. How would I allow my flesh and my pride to be the crown of my own glory, rather than the glory of Christ that abides in me?

"I don't want to see the light of the truth, the Word that contradicts my own carnal mind and my fleshly desires" – excuses!

"I didn't wait on the Lord" – excuses!

"The Lord moves too slowly" – excuses!

"I'm dealing with my feelings right now and will move the way I want to move" – excuses!

I did not to forget the Word and the instructions given to me. I was in the Lord, and in the presence of God while he delivered me from my afflictions of fornication and adultery. The devil teems with evil to destroy the man of God and to discourage the woman of God. God said, "I will turn it into good," and we will receive the wisdom from God.

Lean not unto your own understanding, or that of anyone who does not get his instructions from whom you serve. The Lord showed you what you should do if you want the Word. Our hearing builds on the Word. He's committed in that Word, to love you according to the Spirit, not because of the flesh.

"In the beginning was the Word, and the Word was with God and the Word was God." (John 1:1)

We ask the Lord in the name of Jesus for the divine wisdom, knowledge, and understanding that surpasses all understanding, in the things that concern us. This Divine wisdom, knowledge, and understanding guides us, that we lean not unto our own understanding. The Holy Spirit reveals to us all understanding that is true, that we be not lead in ignorance according to our own understanding.

Our understanding comes from the Lord, our Savior, Jesus Christ, and from his Father who created all things. All things that are created by God were made for him and by him. He made all things, first in the Spirit by the Father in heaven, then manifest on earth through the son, Jesus, in heaven as it is on earth.

In the name of Jesus, we will not have to war with flesh and blood, but with spirits and principalities. How do you fight in war against what you cannot see? In the name of Jesus, for it takes the body of Christ that is Christ Jesus:

Book Two: The Trinity Of God In Man

"This is my flesh, for I have broken it for you. This is my blood – take and drink it, for me and you, and you and me." I am him, and he's in me, for me and my Father are one. If you've seen me, you've seen the Father, for I am one with the Father. "Our Father, who art in heaven, hallowed be thy name. Thy kingdom come, thy will be done, on earth as it is in heaven." (Matthew 6:9)

Who do they say that I am? I have I rebuilt my army and know the mind of God, for you and me, and me and you. Follow me as I follow Christ to be one with him, to be of one mind with Christ, to be even in the body of Christ. He reveals himself to us as the body of Christ, telling us to pray while he watches.

How do we pray if we cannot see him as he sees us? That is faith, the substance of things hoped for. It is in the revelations of the things that are not seen, according to the conscious mind in the name of Jesus. He said, "I am the way, the truth, and the life, for they abide in me and I in them."

I know the secrets, the mysteries of the scripture given to you by my Father in heaven, who reveals them. It is all truth, for my Father loves the Son, and the Son loves the Father. I see my Father in the creation of all the things that I do on Earth. The creation of all things by he who created them, that all things that are invisible are made visible in due time, in due season.

Angels will walk up to me, opening themselves in glory to the Lord. We too are opened up. Behold, the angel of the Lord comes to me in the form of a man. The Lord says, "dance with me – you will see angels ascending and descending upon the son of man, for me and you, and you and me. For this is my body, and this is my blood of the substances of the things hoped for. I will abide in you, in the physical aspect of my body, my blood, my bone."

My flesh will be made perfect in his image that abides in us. The more you have seen, the more you will see. What was invisible is made visible through the Spirit.

The carnal mind manifests itself through the disobedience of man, leading to fornication. Fornication is a demon that manifests itself through action, through the will of the person that brings forth its image. You know what the demon looks like: robbery, murder, rape, and anything that is a transgression of the body.

The word of God says that if any man that lacks wisdom, let him ask of the Father who gives in abundance and upbraideth not. "They abide in me, and I in them, for my Father and I are one. If you have seen me, you've seen my Father. Who do they say that I am? I am that I am. Ask me anything in wisdom, and it will be fully engulfed in the graphic Word of God, entwined to be one with Christ."

Many preachers come up short in the glory of God by trying to preach the Word of God from the outside, interpreting what they feel on the inside because they have not been drawn to witness the things that were on the outside. When we ask God for divine wisdom, knowledge, and understanding, he says,"I will show you the things thereof, even things that eyes have not seen nor ears heard."

These are the heavenly revelations that have been given to us who abide in Christ. They would go before us, to stand and witness the Word of God and behold his face in the name of Jesus. If you were crucified with him, surely you should be able to show the wounds of your crucifixion. If you were raised with him, surely you would be able to show the power of the body, and you and him, for that is the power of Christ. It is a resurrection of faith, a bold faith.

What is bold faith? Bold faith is the insurance of the Word of God. How do we walk in the strength of the Word of God? We walk as one in the mind of Christ, for his one body has many members. He draws all men, carrying us before the Father, advocating before the Father for us, his servants in human bodies.

Anthony Walker

www.ingramcontent.com/pod-product-compliance
Lightning Source LLC
Chambersburg PA
CBHW030350100526
44592CB00010B/901